TO:

FROM:

Copyright © 2010 Hallmark Licensing, Inc.

Published by Hallmark Books,
a division of Hallmark Cards, Inc.,
Kansas City, MO 64141
Visit us on the Web at www.Hallmark.com.

Editor: Theresa Trinder
Art Director: Kevin Swanson
Designer: Mark Voss
Production Artist: Dan Horton
Special thanks to the Hallmark writers
and artists who contributed to this book.

ISBN: 978-1-59530-265-6

BOK2100

Printed and bound in China

THE GUY'S GUIDE

GOOD-TO-KNOWs, HAVE-TO-KNOWs, NO-NO-NOs,
AND OTHER FUNNY, IMPORTANT
(BUT MOSTLY FUNNY) STUFF FOR GUYS.

BY DAN TAYLOR

FOREWARD

by Attila the Hun

As even the quickest glance will indicate, this book gives the reader a layered, complex, and intriguing view of men. This is only appropriate, as men are layered, complex, and intriguing.

Take me for example. You think you know all about me and the Huns. Riding around on horses, taking over nations, torturing enemies, and on and on. But that is just one side of the scroll, as we used to say.

Ever seen my watercolor paintings? Thought not. They are mostly seascapes, but I have experimented with portraits, too. Everyone says they are very good. Yes, bad things happened to one nitpicker who did not say that. I also dabbled in pottery. Mostly by smashing it, but that is how I express myself. Must artists always be misunderstood?

My point is that men are complicated. The idea that we just eat and drink and attack enemies and watch sports while thinking about sex is, frankly, unfair. Sometimes we are not thinking at all.

See what I am saying? Maybe when your village is in ruins, you will get it. Just kidding! Anyway, read the book. Or watch your village burn. Again, I kid! Probably.

ATH

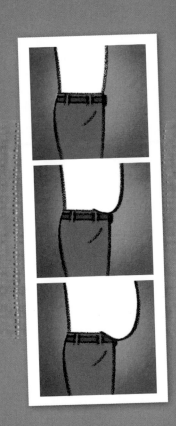

YES, YOU CAN STILL WEAR THE SAME SIZE PANTS YOU DID IN HIGH SCHOOL.

BUT SHOULD YOU? (NO, YOU SHOULD NOT.)

TO TUCK OR NOT TO TUCK?

Can guys have no body image issues? Can they be better adjusted and more evolved than women at even one thing? No. But they can be totally delusional.

Guys are comfortable with their bodies not because their bodies are so great, but because they feel they could be great. Pretty quickly. With very little work.

Ask any guy and he'll tell you he isn't getting bigger. But he is getting better at fooling himself. If the guy in question is wearing a football jersey, he'll tell you it's a way to support his team. Not a way to change a curve into a straight line.

Jerseys don't tuck in. Neither do hooded sweatshirts, camouflage jackets, or suit coats. This works out well for guys from all walks of life. In the last few years, it's been more and more acceptable for guys to wear what used to be called "dress shirts" untucked. And, in the last few years, guys have gotten bigger than ever. (Coincidence?)

In our increasingly clogged hearts, we believe that a few laps around the block, a couple sets of push-ups, a few dozen sit-ups, and it's "Hello, six-pack!" Sure, an actual six-pack is more likely, but that's not the issue. The dream is there, lying in wait, just like the muscles under that layer of protective coating. Any day now. Getting into a routine, hitting the bag, wearing the plastic sweat suit—and look out world!—that guy who never really existed is back!

POP QUIZ

A guy's idea of dressing up is:

☐ a shirt and tie
☐ a shirt and sports coat
☐ a shirt

HAIR TODAY, GONE TOMORROW

Pretending not to care about your hair is critical to guys of almost all ages. When you're three, it's just another place to put your food, but after that—even if you've shaved it all off or buzzed it to almost-shaved-all-off—guys think about it more than they let on.

Here's the breakdown of guys' deepest-secret hair thoughts, by age.

Middle School. How do the other guys on the team have their hair? (Note: Guys "have"—not "do"—their hair; that's girls.) Mohawks? Buzzed? Euro-style long? (Note: Only okay for soccer players.) Do girls like it that way?

High School. How do the other guys on the team/in my classes/at my job have their hair? Do I join in or do I distinguish myself by being different? How different is too different? If all the rebels have the same hair, are they still rebelling? Will my hair effect my chance at scholarships? Do girls like it that way?

College. How do the other guys in the dorm/in the frat/in the band have their hair? I'm not starting to lose it, am I? No, that's crazy talk. How could I be losing my hair? Well, Dad did. Oh, crap! Which dorm/frat/band wears hats? Note to self: research hats. Do girls like them?

25–55. Good thing I enjoy golf/hunting/fishing, because everybody's wearing hats while golfing/hunting/fishing! Do girls like golfing/hunting/fishing?

56–Death. Finally, I don't have to pretend not to care what my hair looks like. Except I kind of still do. How do the other guys at the office/clubhouse/nursing home have theirs? Do any of them have any at all? Do girls like scalps?

Bob soon realized that his hair peninsula had broken off to form its own island.

VINCE LEARNS THE DANGERS
OF TAKING HAIR-GROWTH PILLS
AND POTENCY PILLS
AT THE SAME TIME.

THREE BEST THINGS ABOUT SHAVING YOUR HEAD:

1. Popular style of beloved pro athletes.

2. People assume you are not bald and can grow hair back anytime.

3. No more expensive visits to barber.

THREE WORST THINGS ABOUT SHAVING YOUR HEAD:

1. Tempting area for later regretted tattoo.

2. Must readjust your entire baseball cap collection.

3. Shaving reveals your head is shaped like a green pepper.

MAN CANNOT LIVE BY BEER ALONE.

(BEER AND PRETZELS, MAYBE. BUT NOT BEER ALONE.)

ONE TEQUILA, TWO TEQUILA, THREE TEQUILA . . . OK, THAT'S ENOUGH

Drinking is (or was) a foundational part of being a guy. This, however, does not mean that all guys must drink. You just have to have a guy-approved excuse.

For example, if someone offers you a beer and you say, "No, thanks, I'm watching my weight," that's not good. Instead consider, "No, thanks, I've got a fight coming up. Sure, it's just my local boxing club, but when there's eleven hundred dollars on the line, well, I want to be in the best shape of my life." Note the eleven hundred. When pulling numbers out of your ass, it is wise to not make up too small an amount, or too large, or too rounded-off.

If that's too much to remember, you can go with: "My lawyers have advised me against any kind of drinking right now." The plural is key here. One lawyer sounds made up. Several lawyers—perhaps some sort of legal team—sounds cool. Sounds like you've seen trouble, and that's what you want. You want to look like you're not drinking because of trouble. Trouble you don't want to explain. Trouble nobody wants a piece of.

If you are going to drink, there are ways to ace and ways to fail. Wine, for example, is tricky. You don't want to know too much about it because you'll sound like you've tied a sweater around your neck and are looking for a picnic. But—and this is important—one guy knows wine and knows it well. That's Bond. And Bond is a guy of guys. We've included a handy list of drinks that are always okay, drinks that are borderline, and drinks that are always no, no, no. Memorize this list and you'll be fine. And, if you can't remember the list, well, you've had enough.

NEVER OK

- Champagne (even if it's brut)
- Mojito
- Any kinds of martini that Bond hasn't ordered
- Wine that requires French accent to say properly
- Anything that's "Lite," "Light," "Lyte," or "Ultra"
- Flavored beer, especially fruit
- Any kind of "Cooler"
- Anything with an umbrella
- Shots with cute, suggestive names

ALWAYS OK

- Domestic beer
- Whiskey (because of cowboys)
- Anything served in a hollowed-out horn of a dead animal that used to have horns
- Anything served in a hollowed-out anything
- Any/all "body shots"
- Anything set on fire
- Beer you made yourself
- Any kind of alcohol you made yourself
- Shots with cute, suggestive names if served by crazy hot waitress

DON'T

1. Get drunk and have your appendix removed in Mexico.

2. Get excited if the cops say they're taking you to the "Drunk Tank." It's not a hip new bar.

3. Drunk-dial the girl who gave you a hickey in the tenth grade and ask if she's, like, married.

DO

Avoid flirting when drunk. Alcohol may impair your ability to operate a pick-up line.

1. "I see you and me growing old together . . . or your friend over there, either one."

2. "There's more to me than drinking in bars. I also drink at home."

3. "Can I have your boob number? I mean your phone boob?"

4. "I want to buy you a drink. Can I borrow ten dollars?"

5. I want to hear your hopes and dreams... after I go vomit."

6. "Wanna come home with me? I'll tell my mom to clear out."

NOTHIN' COULD
BE FINER THAN
TO BE IN YOUR
RECLINER.

TOP TEN AREAS A MAN CAN CONTROL IN HIS OWN HOUSE

10. Basement

9. Garage

8–1. Um, that's it, really. Just two. If a man has no basement, he can sometimes get access to the less-desirable parts of the crawl spaces. But if there is no garage, he will not have any authority over the carport. Zero. Probably can't even park his own car. Also, some guys who work from home will get limited input on an office. The accepted themes here will be "Golf" and "Ducks," usually in decoy form. Must be one or the other. Ducks playing golf is too much.

THE DAY YOU
DON'T GET
ASKED TO HELP
SOMEONE MOVE
IS KIND OF A
SAD DAY.

BUT ONLY A LITTLE BIT SAD.

UNDERNEATH IT ALL
(The Basement)

You think you can finish your basement, but unless your basement is already finished except for, like, a throw rug, you can't. And you probably shouldn't be trusted to choose a throw rug. (It's a misnomer— they're not for throwing.)

Basements look like they can be great do-it-yourself projects because they are usually not huge and they are, typically, under the house. This leads to the false sense that it is not a big deal. Since it's under the house, no one will know if anything goes wrong.

But you'll know. And it'll haunt you. You'll toss and turn, you'll have bad dreams. Dreams where your drop ceiling actually drops. You'll confess to strangers that you're pretty sure some of the studs are not "sixteen on center." You'll wonder where that wire came from and where it's going. (What if it's a really important wire?!)

You'll hear about a fire on the news and you'll be pretty sure they did exactly what you just did, and now look. The news crew is all over the front yard and a neighbor kid is crying because Li'l Furball is missing and it smells like roasted hamster outside. That could be your house! You better not finish your basement unless you're so confident that you haven't read this far. But if you have read this far, don't finish your basement! It will finish you.

On the other hand, if you have a friend you can lean on to "help" you finish the basement, this is the best-case scenario. He can do all the brain work while you drink beer. Also, even though he's doing all the work, you'll still need to buy lots of tools. Fancy ones. Complicated ones. Tools you don't really begin to understand, but are shiny and loud and require massive battery packs. You may even need a truck.

HOW A WOMAN SEES IT:

HOW A MAN SEES IT:

Sea Spray → ← GREEN

Garden Moss → ← GREEN

Very Verde → ← GREEN

Jana

32

"Men and cable go together
like women and . . .
whatever it is women like."

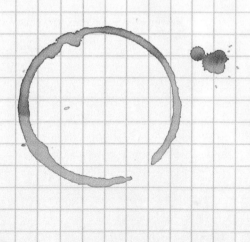

CAVE DWELLING

If a man is lucky enough to have a basement, or a big garage, or maybe an attic, he can sometimes "decorate" it as he wants. Except he can't call it "decorating." He can "fix it up" like he wants. "Fixing up" is OK because it's got "fixing" right in the name. So, if he's fortunate enough to get a fix-it-up space for himself, here are the essential elements, in order of importance . . .

Big-Screen TV:
"Big" is a relative term. Of course we all dream of a world where every man has his own 72 inches of diagonal plasma real estate. But in reality, it's just important that it be bigger than a TV in, say, the kitchen.

Beer Fridge:
Again, size is relative. Ideally, this will be an old refrigerator that is regulation (house) size. It should have a broken handle that has been duct-taped on and possibly several NASCAR stickers on it (the whole thing, not just the handle). If it appears to have been shot at, that's a bonus, especially if it looks like it was hit with buckshot. But if need be, a college-dorm-size is better than nothing. In fact, in a weird twist of square footage, a smaller fridge that might have seen some dorm time is better than a bigger fridge that looks like it should be in a French or English apartment. Euro fridges are for Euros. American fridges are way big or way small—never in between.

Recliner:
Preferably broken and not matching anything. Bonus points if it smells like dog. Especially if you don't have a dog. A worn-out spot on the armrest that goes all the way to the wood is a good place to set a beer, so bonus if you've got one of those.

Art:

This falls into three distinct categories and gives the man a chance to fix the place up in a way that reflects his personal tastes, interests, and insane/rabid passions. Namely: sports teams, swimsuit models, and cars. (Note: Degrees of interest and/or insane/rabid passion for each of the three categories will vary.)

Another TV:

This should be obvious. What if something happens to the first TV? This is why hospitals have generators. Hope for the best, prepare for the worst. You learned this in Boy Scouts.

Another Beer Fridge:

See above.

THE SIZE OF YOUR TV
IS NOT A MEASURE OF
YOUR SUCCESS.
IT'S THE QUALITY OF
YOUR FRIENDSHIPS.

AND HOW BIG YOUR
FRIEND'S TV IS.

Betty often wondered if it was too obvious her husband decorated the house.

Rednecks on a Saturday Night

THE COOLEST WAY TO GET TO THE EMERGENCY ROOM:

CARS, TRUCKS, AND POWER TOOLS

TEN THINGS ALL GUYS WISH THEY HAD
WHETHER THEY NEED THEM OR NOT

1. Chainsaw
2. Wood chipper
3. Semitruck horn
4. Semitruck
5. Sliding door with retinal scan
6. Tiger
7. Credit card with razor-sharp edges (for throwing and decapitating)
8. Swiss bank account (but not for the money, just 'cause it's cool)
9. Wine cellar in cave (again, not for the wine)
10. Bigger chainsaw than original chainsaw ("The Upgrade")

The Internet? Bah!
Back in the the olden days,
if you wanted to see a picture
of a naked lady on a new truck
you had to make an EFFORT!

SPEAKING OF TRUCKS

It's always a good idea for a guy to have a truck or a motorcycle, or both if there's room in the garage and the budget. When/if the Lord has answered your prayers and you own a truck, it's best for it to have as many as possible of the following:

- Tool box
- Off-road tires
- Gun rack
- AM-only radio
- Bench seat
- Rust
- Decal that says how much you like your dog, or shooting at things, or how much you don't like trucks that are not your truck
- Case of beer in bed
- Worn-through place in floorboard
- Trailer hitch
- Winch
- Drinkin' buddy
- Woman who is not repulsed by truck

SEVEN GREAT EXCUSES FOR NOT HAVING A COOL CAR

1. You need the money for food and stuff.

2. You're not a middle-aged balding guy compensating for anything.

3. Would look weird with your "In case of Rapture, car will be unmanned" bumper sticker.

4. Tough enough to keep women off you as it is.

5. What? A Prius isn't cool?

6. Bo and Luke Duke didn't even need car doors.

7. BMW doesn't have a model that runs on leftover oil from your deep fryer.

SPEAKING OF MOTORCYCLES

We were not speaking of motorcycles. But we are now.

And all you have to remember is this: crotch-rocket bikes are for kids. Which makes Harleys, of course, the only real choice. After that, you get into the clothing issue. A black t-shirt with the logo of a shop that's a long ride from where you live is good, boots that look like they double as brakes are good, and a jacket (as long as it's for show and not for warmth) is good.

Jackets with fringe are borderline, and chaps . . . well, if you think you're a guy who can wear fringe and chaps to a biker bar, even a suburban biker bar, you go right ahead. Good luck.

Also, if you have a headset so that you can talk to your wife or girlfriend, who is literally on your back for a long cross-country trip, well, maybe didn't get the point of the bike in the first place.

THINGS YOU DON'T WANT TO HEAR WHILE GETTING A TATTOO

- "Eagle? I thought you said beagle."
- "There are two o's in Bob, right?"
- "We're all out of red, so I used fuchsia."
- "Damn hiccups."
- "Anything else you want to say? You've got plenty of room back here."
- "I'll bet you can't tell I've never done this before."
- "The flag's all done and, you know, the folds of fat make a nice waving effect."

Shortly after the first hammer was invented,
the first cuss word was invented.

TEN THINGS NO GUY WILL EVER ASK
ABOUT A POWER TOOL

1. How does it work?

2. Why do I need it?

3. Is protective eyewear required?

4. Does it come with instructions?

5. Is it available in seafoam green?

6. Can I use it to open bottles? (Assume you can.)

7. Couldn't I save money by renting one instead?

8. Is it dangerous?

9. Is there a smaller, less powerful option?

10. Does it make my butt look big?

THERE IS NO "I"
IN "MODERATION,"
EXCEPT AT THE END,
WHERE YOU HARDLY
NOTICE IT.

HOT ENOUGH FOR YA?

Some people grill chickens, and even seafood, while tailgating. There's nothing wrong with this, of course, if the tails they are gating are parked at a garden show, or a craft fair, or possibly a renaissance festival. But at a football game, of course, it's clearly wrong.

You can grill steaks. You can grill any/all random meats in casings, which covers brats, dogs, Polish, etc. Ribs are OK, and even some chili is OK, as long as it's hot enough to literally grill itself.

Everything else is wrong, unless, again, you're at one of those venues mentioned above. (Though now that we think about it, most renaissance festivals have those giant turkey legs, and that's an okay substitute, but only if it's truly massive and has tendons and sinews and grease dripping from it, and only if you've got a battle axe in your other hand.)

Extra points for grilling on a barrel of some sort that you have sawed open yourself and ignited with some kind of totally illegal portable bomb. And—this should go without saying—the stuff left on the grill from last time is the secret ingredient for this time. It should be noted that some guys will grill vegetables. Some guys also get manicures; it doesn't make it okay.

DO

be creative with food

Meat Lover's Cake

DON'T
be too creative

Remember:

Food isn't love.
 Love is fickle.
Food is always there.

Where the Trouble Begins

RELATIONSHIPS, THE MOST DANGEROUS SHIPS.

(EXCEPT FOR NUCLEAR SUBS. WITH NUCLEAR WEAPONS.)

TOP TEN MOST MYSTERIOUS MYSTERIES ABOUT WOMEN

Women are mysterious. This is by design, because where there is mystery, there is unlimited interest. The Internet has helped make a dent in the infinite list of stuff guys don't know, but still, most mysteries remain unsolved.

Here are, as it turns out, the Top Ten.

1. How they can tell the differences between a dozen kinds of lettuce
2. How they can talk to their mom on the phone for a whole hour even though nothing has happened since last time they talked
3. How they can think "sports are stupid" yet be attracted to jocks (who are stupid)
4. How they can be so nice to people they so hate
5. How they can smell so good, like, all the time
6. How they can never remember that there's always a game on, every week
7. How they can tell if you vacuumed around everything instead of underneath everything
8. How they can tell if you're on the computer while you're on the phone
9. How they always leave you with the sense that they have "let" you do whatever it is you just did
10. How they can tell all the sexy vampire books apart

Craig didn't see how
"getting into a woman's pants"
was any kind of a challenge.

HOW TO BE A SENSITIVE GUY

When you talk to a woman, just say what you'd usually say, but replace the word "sports" with "our relationship."

"Our relationship is very important to me. Sorry, I get a little emotional when I think about our relationship."

Exception to rule: "Wanna drink some beer, invite the guys over, and talk about our relationship?"

Ideal Woman #111

Is convinced that your
boss is an idiot who
can't see your genius
and she speaks
another language when
she's really mad.

Quell'uomo
è irritante
me!

Ideal Woman #309

Thinks "Freebird" is too short
and that throw pillows are
a ridiculous waste of money.

RELATIONSHIP DO'S AND DON'TS

DON'T describe your spouse as your better half and make quote marks around "better."
DO consider your partner's tastes before committing to a 12-month calendar.

DON'T assume a heart-shaped tattoo with her initials on it counts as a romantic gift.
DO remove the secret videos after watching them.

DON'T give her sexy underwear as a gag gift.
DO check state laws before bringing home an exotic pet.

IF SHE FALLS DOWN
AND YOU LAUGH
AFTER YOU FIND OUT
THAT'S SHE'S OK, YOU
CAN BE PRETTY SURE
THAT SHE'S THE ONE.

★#⚡@!
THAT'S IT. THE KIDS AREN'T ALLOWED TO WATCH SPORTS WITH YOU ANYMORE.
brian.

LOVE & MARRIAGE (& KIDS?!?)

Most guys are familiar with the good things about being single.
But there are some good things about being married, too.
Here they are.

One: You've got a better chance at having a lawn. Many guys feel
you're not really a man until you have one. "The lawn" will give you
endless things to talk about with other guys in the neighborhood.
You can talk about the weather and how it might affect the lawn, and
the neighbor's dog and how that affects the lawn. You can talk about
various types of grass and their relative merits for your part of the
hemisphere. Mowers, all by themselves, are endlessly fascinating.
If you have a rider, well, there's 45 minutes of standing-around-talk-
ing-about-it right there, and if you don't, maybe one of your neighbors
will. Maybe it will be that jerk with the dog. You can waste another
15 minutes on him and there you go, there's an hour of guy bonding
and healthy human interaction, brought to you by your lawn.

Two: You might have children. There are some challenges here,
of course, and your lawn may suffer, but once they get here, the real
advantages begin. Kids start off life very small and rather dumb.
Which gives you a status that can't be duplicated anywhere else.
Your kids will think you're the biggest, strongest, smartest, bravest,
fill-in-the-blankest guy in the world. Then they'll turn five. But in the
meantime, you'll see where that "King of the Castle" thing comes
from. Have some fun with it. Make some stuff up. It's not going to
last forever.

TOP TEN THINGS HUSBANDS SHOULD HAVE NOTICED WITHOUT BEING TOLD

1. Subtle changes in hair (color, style, length, sheen, bounciness, etc.)
2. The way the (doesn't matter what) brings out her eyes
3. The new black dress (not to be confused with all the other black dresses, no matter how many there seem to be)
4. The way your mom didn't say anything about the salad, after specifically asking that she bring salad
5. How the other soccer parents don't slice the oranges properly
6. Clear signals from the teacher that your child is exceptional
7. Balsamic reduction glaze and how it's much different than regular balsamic glaze
8. How cute the waitress is (Trick item! You were not supposed to notice that.)
9. That her cookies were by far the best cookies at the bake sale
10. That she didn't eat any of the cookies at the bake sale (You had twelve.)

YOUR SCORE DOESN'T
REALLY MATTER,
AS LONG AS IT'S BETTER
THAN EVERYONE ELSE'S.

GOLF IS FOR SWINGERS

Why golf? Simple. If a guy asks another guy, "Would you like to go for a walk in a field, since it's such a nice day?" that guy will be, at best, shunned. But . . . if that same guy says, "Look at that sun! Let's get out and play a round or two," you might hug him. And that would be okay. (In some regions, you'll see the same with hunting. If you said, "Let's get up really early, dress alike, and stand very still in the woods together, even though it is six degrees out," you might get shot. But "Let's go deer hunting" will make you friends for life.)

Should you walk or should you get a cart or should you split the difference and use a battery-powered, self-propelled bag/dolly kind of thing? The answer is simple. Can you afford a cart? Then use one. Can you afford a bag-dolly thing? Then use one. Can you afford a robot that actually plays for you while you watch from the clubhouse? Then good luck, Robot!

Technically speaking, it's not legal to gamble on golf, so we're not going to condone or even joke about it, because it's illegal. It's also really the only reason to play golf, but we're not going to mention it. In fact, you can bet we won't say another word about it. Because betting is illegal. (But we totally won, so pay up.)

You can get around the illegality by betting for things instead of for money. You could, say, bet a beer-a-hole. Or fifty dollars worth of beer-a-hole. Or one hundred dollars (worth of beer)-a-hole. That kind of thing.

The pros put their pants
on one leg at a time.
They're just way nicer pants.

The 18th hole at Fantasy Golf Camp.

TOP TEN GOLF EXCUSES

1. "I was thinking about 'Nam. We lost a lot of men . . .
   a lot of good men."

2. Old football injury acting up

3. New football injury acting up

4. Worn out by Bulgarian supermodels

5. "Stupid weather satellite!"

6. Barometric pressure (alone, or as part of satellite excuse)

7. Couldn't find lucky ball

8. Couldn't find lucky hat

9. Can't putt without miniature windmill

10. Extra strokes mean more golf for the money

TOP TEN THINGS TO YELL AT THE RADIO DURING A SPORTS SHOW

1. "Idiot!"
2. "Homer!"
3. "Front-runner!"
4. "Fair-weather Fan!"
5. "Bandwagoner!"
6. "Grandstander!"
7. "Front-office Hack!"
8. "Media Hack!"
9. "Front-office Media Hack!"
10. "Free Bird!" (Just always appropriate to yell.)

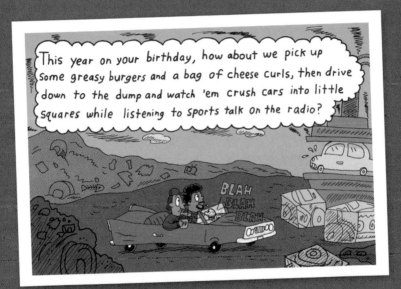

BEST SPORTS RADIO CALL-IN QUESTION EVER

Would you rather be Michael Jordan for thirty days or Brett Favre
for thirty days (if Brett had won two Super Bowls)? Or . . . would
you rather be invisible and all-knowing for a week and a half or would
you rather be an adjustable lens at an "SI" Swimsuit Issue shoot?

SECOND-BEST SPORTS RADIO CALL-IN QUESTION EVER

Could the coach of (your college team here) coach five bears
(brown or grizzly) to beat a team of ninjas in a half-court game
to twenty-one, if the bears had jet packs and the ninjas were
blindfolded and the coach already had one technical against him?

Cheerleading is the most
dangerous of all high school
sports. The risks include
broken bones, internal
injuries, and, if you're a
male cheerleader, several
severe wedgies a day.

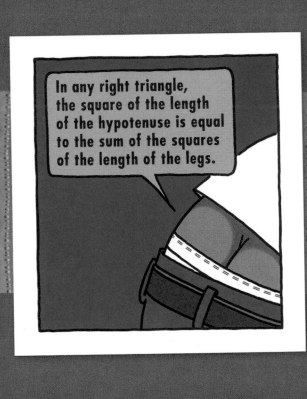

THE VERY MANY EMOTIONS OF GUYS . . .

AND OTHER WISECRACKS

TOP TEN THINGS GUYS HAVE TROUBLE ADMITTING

1. Crying (except during sporting events)
2. Knowing the difference between white and off-white
3. Pre-crying sniffles
4. Kind of not liking "Extra Hot Death Sauce" on burrito
5. Crying because of "Extra Hot Death Sauce" on burrito
6. Having a favorite flower
7. Giggling and/or being touched emotionally during "Gilmore Girls"
8. Giggling and/or being touched emotionally any other time
9. Eye-corner moisture that could lead to pre-cry sniffle
10. Crying (during sporting events, but when other guys are not)

GUY OF GUYS: MOVIE VERSION

There are lots of great scenes of guys being guys in exemplary ways throughout cinematic history. John Wayne pretty much any time he was on screen. Likewise, Steve McQueen. Jack Palance. Sean Connery. Clint Eastwood. You know what I mean.

But there's a scene in a recent movie that set a bar for all other guys in movies and it holds its own (no pun intended) against any that came before.

In 2007's "Eastern Promises," Viggo Mortensen plays a Russian gangster. As often happens in gangster movies, he has a conflict with other gangsters. This makes it seem more fair. If Viggo had a conflict with the cable guy, like most of us, he'd seem like a really scary bully. But as it is, this is gangster-on-gangster and no one minds that.

So, he's in a Turkish bath, because (again, as often happens in gangster movies) this is supposed to be a safe place where you can't wear a wire. You can wear a towel and nothing else. That's what Viggo's got on, just a towel.

Then (and you really have to see it to appreciate it) two big guys walk in wearing real clothes and sporting curved knives. For some reason, the curved knife seems much scarier than the straight, pointy kind, even though that's not really logical.

What can Viggo do? Run? Hide? How about go ahead and fight the two guys, even if it means he'll lose the towel and (except for his elaborate tattoos) be buck naked and (one would assume) really slippery.

Next time you're in a steam room in a towel, pick any two guys and imagine how you'd do against them if they had clothes on. Now give them curved knives. Now make them professional killers, sent to kill you. Guy of guys.

A giant alien *battles* a monster truck, while two girls in bikinis have a slow-motion fight under a lawn sprinkler, as the hometown team finally wins it all.

GUY OF GUYS: REAL LIFE VERSION

Yes, you got your sports heroes. Your war heroes. Your superheroes. But this guy, while actually belonging to a subset of sports hero, is not a seven-foot-tall, 300-hundred-pound behemoth; he's a fairly regular guy who did the most guyish guy thing in the history of guyhood.

And theoretically, a woman could do the same thing. This wasn't competitive mustache growing or something (though, in all fairness, there are women who could compete there, too). This was pure guts. Some of which stayed behind in the rocks.

Here's the headline, from a "National Geographic" article at the time:

In April 2003, climber Aron Ralston entered Utah's Bluejohn Canyon only to become trapped when an 800-pound boulder shifted, crushed his hand, and pinned him to the canyon wall. For six days, Ralston struggled to free himself while warding off dehydration and hypothermia.

Trapped and facing certain death, Ralston chose a final option that later made him an international sensation: Using a multitool, the climber amputated his right hand, then rappelled to freedom.

"Warding off dehydration and hypothermia"? Most of us can't ward off the flu. If someone sneezes on the elevator, most guys I know give them a look that says something like, "thanks for giving me your cooties." And here's a question and answer that takes the whole thing into the guy-o-sphere: The answer seems obvious, but . . . did it hurt? Here's what he had to say:

> Well, I didn't have any sensation in my right hand from the time of the accident onward. However, I did feel pain coming from the area where the boulder rested on my wrist. When I amputated, I felt every bit of it. It hurt to break the bone, and it certainly hurt to cut the nerve. But cutting the muscle was not as bad.

That's it. Case closed. At least, let's say, for now.

Nature's Musings:
The male inchworm
has got to be bummin'.

If your band hasn't
made it yet,
your band isn't
going to make it.

THE guyPOD PLAYLIST

Just Fine
Metallica
Stones
Zeppelin
Anything ever played in a football stadium
Skynyrd

Borderline
Radiohead
Coldplay
Eagles
John Mayer (blues stuff only)
Dave Matthews Band

Never, Ever
Anyone who was on American Idol, even the "rockers"
Elton John (except for "Saturday Night's Alright for Fighting")
Anything ever played in a soccer stadium
Indigo Girls
Depeche Mode (if you even know who Depeche Mode is, you may
have a problem)

QUESTIONS GUYS SHOULD ASK THEMSELVES, ANSWERED WITH OTHER QUESTIONS

Q: Should I go naked in the gym steam room?
A: Are you in the Russian mafia? Otherwise, no.

Q: Should I bet Charles Barkley $200,000 on this next hole?
A: Are you Michael Jordan? Otherwise, no.

Q: Should I get an earring?
A: Are you a pirate? Otherwise, no.

Q: Should I believe this single woman's online profile?
A: Single? Woman?

Q: Should I sign the papers for this interest-only boat loan?
A: Are you planning on operating heavy machinery? Because you're clearly high.

Q: Can I still wear clothes I wore in high school?
A: Are you still in high school? Otherwise, no.

TOP TEN GUY SUPERSTITIONS

1. Lucky underwear.

2. Sweet-talking an old car will make it start/run better.

3. Sweet-talking bowling ball will make it roll better.

4. The team plays harder because they somehow know you are on the couch wearing their jersey.

5. Catching fish is the result of the strict following of some ritual.

6. Not having to pay for beer consumed while fishing is the result of the strict following of some ritual.

7. Parking in same spot and eating same food while tailgating guarantees team will win.

8. Not having to pay for beer consumed while tailgating is the result of the strict following of some ritual.

9. Lucky shirt will guarantee . . . well, it's just lucky, is all.

10. Lucky hat will cause onlookers to assume it covers full head of hair.

THE THREE COM-MAN-MENTS

1. A man shall not notice another man's haircut, new pants, or recent weight loss.
2. A man shall not ever describe anything as "cute."
3. A man shall not have another man's call identified on his cell phone by a particular ringtone.

We know, we know. Most guys don't like talking about their feelings. We thank you for being one of those guys.

But if you have something you'd like to, you know, get off your hairy, muscular chest, like how hard the coffee came out of your nose when you laughed at our jokes, well, I guess that would be OK.

Hallmark Book Feedback
P.O. Box 419034
Mail Drop 215
Kansas City, MO 64141

booknotes@hallmark.com